"Sales Wizardry: Unlocking Sales Potential"

Willard T. Lewis

TABLE OF CONTENTS

INTRODUCTION

Welcome to the dazzling universe of "Deals Wizardry: Unlocking Deals Potential"! Get ready to leave on a mysterious excursion where you will figure out how to charm outsiders and release your business abilities to their maximum capacity.

In this book, we'll plunge into the specialty of impact, helping areas of strength for you to effect and change even the most wary conceivable outcomes. You'll figure out some way to make a mind-boggling bargain that leaves pariahs craving what you offer as real value. In like manner, we'll examine the meaning of building dependability and supporting relationships with your leads, getting ready for long-term accomplishment.

By the way, it doesn't end there! We'll bounce into the area of fruitful correspondence, outfitting you with the capacities to partake in persuading bargaining conversations that leave a lasting impact. You will likewise figure out how to utilize innovation to get around impediments and transform difficulties into once-in-a-lifetime kinds of chances.

You will figure out how to close arrangements with artfulness and how to scale your deal endeavors for long-term development as you progress through these pages. At the point when you show up at the last area, you'll have embraced your internal arrangements wizard, ready to conquer the arrangements scene with conviction and allure.

Along these lines, get your wand and residue off your shroud, and together, we should go on this astounding excursion. Plan to open up your arrangement potential and become a real arrangement wizard!

CHAPTER 1

GETTING A HANDLE ON THE POSSIBILITY OF BUSINESS

In this current reality, we have been hearing this term" Business", yet paying little mind to harmonious emphasis, it really is supposedly a nonstop issue for by far most business people.

What is business now?

The word business has different delineations. It insinuates confederations that change work and particulars not entirely settled to make an increase on the trade. However, while not-for-profits have all the advantage in achieving communicated targets or further creating establishments, If this advantage is returned to possessors, the business is known as a for-profit business. A couple of associations are state-guaranteed. Most associations are typically guaranteed furtively, yet colossal, strong confederations may be recorded on the financial market and moved by' the public, in that anyone is permitted to participate in the association. The word business is derived from the word' involve,' i.e., business is helpful development.

Associations are a huge wellspring of financial turn of events, which stem generally from a development in effectiveness. One of the huge targets for confederations is a development in productivity, achieved in colorful ways, including the preface of able advancement. The word business likewise suggests the perpendicular business where confederations work, as in the music business.' It can also be used in emulsion construction to portray how important exertion is when working in a particular perpendicular, e.g., agribusiness. The movement of associations is portrayed by business guidelines, which are veritably much like the plan of business power. Trials are one of the most notable feathers of business; they are portrayed by the limited liability of the possessors in that the association has its own real character. The legitimacy of this review, which analyzes business personhood, is being referred to. Colorful kinds of business structures consolidate cooperatives, confederations, and sole effects.

A business can be portrayed as a cooperative or bold element that partakes in mastery, business, or current conditioning. There can be different types of associations depending on various factors. Some are for-profit, while some are non-profit. Also, their power likewise makes them not original to each other. In this case, there are sole effects, confederations, and associations, and that's only the launch.

Business is also the undertakings and conditioning of a person who's making particulars or offering associations with the arrangement to vend them for benefit.

Kinds of Associations

Colorful associations are composed of a dynamic frame or association, or some likeness thereof. In these associations, the positions have a standard impact and commitment.   As indicated by business description, we see that different kinds of associations are:

- **Sole Possession:**

In this kind of business, a lone employee owns and works the business. There is not any kind of genuine separation between the proprietor and the business. Likewise, the onus of genuine notwithstanding trouble liability is on the proprietor.

- **Affiliation:**

As the name suggests, it's a business where no less than two people run it together. The sidekicks get coffers and plutocrats, and a while later, the proponents of the advantage or reversal are insulated among them.

- **Association:**

Around then, a social occasion of individualities acting together has substance. The possessors in this business are called fiscal backers. They look at their points of view on the typical mound of the association. There are unpropitious duty multifariousness rules in an association for business people.

- **Confined Commitment Association (LLC):**

It is not as old as the other business structures. It mixes an association's pass-through charge multiplicity benefits with an undertaking's confined liability benefits.

DIFFERENT SIZES OF BUSINESS

There are different sizes of business

- **Nonpublic trials:**

Are associations where little possessors(an individual or a little assembly) work. For example, family cafés, apparel associations, intimately arranged associations, and conveying associations In this kind of business, the advantages aren't that high anyway, barely enough to continue with the business errands.

- **Moderate measured Business:**

These associations troll in extraordinary multitudinous bones in pay. Generally speaking, it goes from$ 50 million to$ 1 billion. They're spread out better varied with a intimately possessed business. The delegate base of these associations goes from 100 to 999 people.

- **Colossal Business:**

This kind of business naturally fills in as an association. It has a delegate base of 1000 people, and its pay creation is further than$ 1 billion. Regularly, these associations issue commercial stock to support their undertakings. meetly, it's public. In this way, it ought to give a record of unequivocal effects and work constraints. This is an contrary thing to a nonpublic bid, where errands are liberated from controllers.

Undertakings

There are different ways in which associations work. A particular association can portray its business through that particular business. For example, there are adventures in land, agribusiness, publicizing, banking, and more in which associations live. It's because habitually, the term' business' trades with the regular exercises and the outright enhancement of the association.

Different associations in the world have colorful associations and effects. The stylish ones include

- Amazon

The topmost web-based retailer, Amazon, sells a wide grouping of products on its web business stage. It began as an electronic book retailer and got principally every retail order. It also offers circulated figuring associations, film and show streaming stages, and registration effects.

- Apple

It's a recognized association notable for its innovative electronic effects. They vend laptops, mobile phones, earphones, watches, and computers. Principally, they likewise offer colorful feathers of help like music, videotape, and electronic and creation associations.

- Walmart

Being one of the most stylish retailers generally, Walmart is a worldwide company that runs a chain of hypermarkets offering an enormous grouping of goods, going from family dress to housewares. It's accessible in 24 countries and has a considerable number of delegates from all over the world.

Before starting a business, what should you do?

One must take different paths before starting a business.

First and foremost, one should lead the demand disquisition and develop a strategy.

The next step ought to be to search for capital or other backing and choose a position and business structure.

It's also essential to pick the right name, complete the selection connection, and get the commitment reports and top awards. Before starting a business, it's plainly necessary to have a fiscal balance. How should one start an online business? An electronic business is not exactly a customary business. You need to design your point after requesting exploration, seductive methodology enhancement, and nonsupervisory work customs.

From that point on, you should start taking pitfalls with your objective supplication and use online entertainment venues to attract your group. What's field- tried procedure? seductive ways help with keeping up with your business and secure the resource mentioned to start the exercises. Traditional field- tested strategy or further marketable strategy are the two options. The history is piled with nuances like the association's summary, plan for progress, thing information, deals protrusions, etc.

A conclusive one is not unreasonably organized at this point and has significant information like nuances of the investment, cost structure, and benefit water frame, and that's only the launch.

THE THREE FARTHEST RUNG OF BUSINESS SORTING OUT

This is an   inconceivable snare of people, processes, considerations, history, and, in this manner, basically more. It's consequently precious to have a structure for getting our arms around it. The three limits of business understanding are the frame I use. These three restrictions do not do much to separate and organize the business; a useful introductory model can do that. It's also important that they tell inside story of the business.

- **The Business/ Benefit Model**

The business/ benefit model identifies the primary benefit drivers for the association. These are the three limitations of business understanding. It gives information on the association among pay and costs, how they relate to the association's errands, and in the long run, what effects and associations are by and large useful. It highlights plutocrats advantages and burdens. Different associations could work in a similar general deal space, but their specific game plan and help motorists shift significantly.

- **The Functioning Model of the Business:** Nearly associated with the morning assiduity and advantage model is the performing model. The performing model is an issue of some significance in the straightforward, working shoot out of the Business/ Advantage Model we have as of late covered. Still, your company's functional model encompasses more than just that. The performing model encompasses your association's perspective, approach, and styles of action. In the end, the working model explains how your association exceptionally finishes products.

- **The Merciless Position:**

The last element of business understanding is serious arranging. Serious situating demonstrates how well-prepared and organized your company is to support and distribute callers rather than its rivals.

WHY ARE THESE THREE POINTS SO CRITICAL?

Information on your cooperation's Plan of Action, Working Model, and Serious Sticking positions you to manage the elderly administration of your relationship as a friend who's in contact with the main corridor of the business, from M&A sweats to working fabric overhauls. By learning about these three restrictions, you can get beyond an introductory understanding of business operations and into the core of the association. You put yourself in the stylish possible position to impact your musketeers and associates by clinging to these three limits of business understanding because you'll be speaking from the same perspective as them. Instructions for" Chancing the Business" in Step- by- Step Forms Take the necessary way to gain a solid understanding of your company's strategy,   functional model, and competitive position. Read your association's entire fiscal report's and design.

- Get duplicates of your   realistic and authentic reports overall.
- Read pundit reports, spots, and exchange journals. Go to mind social affairs.
- Join peer social affairs.
- Gain explanation on many points.

Know your company and its working model. In the long run, come a devoted supporter of your association's serious arranging. It's likely going to   stand out prominently in your search for relationships. With your recently secured data on the three limits of business seeing hard, you're ready to put them to work in your approaching sweats to shape and vend your fashion.

CHAPTER 2

COMPREHENSION OF THE BUSINESS ENVIRONMENT

What exactly is the business environment?

All of the factors that have an effect on a business make up a business environment. Employees and resources, for example, are examples of internal factors, while customers and markets are examples of external factors.

What are the kinds of business conditions?

Here are a portion of the normal kinds of business conditions:

- **Monetary:**

A company's potential impact on the global and local economies is known as its economic environment. This can incorporate elements like financial circumstances, remembering per capita pay for your objective market, or greater monetary frameworks, for example, in the event that a business works in an entrepreneurial or communist society. While assessing your financial business climate, you should seriously think about spending patterns, expansion rates, and development rates to assist you in determining how you could market and sell your items.

- **Sociocultural:**

An organization's sociocultural climate includes the qualities of individuals in a particular market, similar to socioeconomics and cultural jobs. You should seriously mull over angles like your clients' convictions, language, education, and future while finding out about this climate. Each of these could decide how you could arrive at explicit clients or how they could draw in with your image. For instance, if a relational peculiarity changes and it's more normal for families to have one kid instead of two, you should seriously mull over what this could mean for your promotion.

Sociocultural business climate model

As additional organizations offer adaptable work courses of action, customer needs for at-home items like PCs, work seats, and work areas increase. Clients bound to buy supplies like work sacks, screen protectors, and dividers are presently purchasing items to change in accordance with the accepted practices of working at home. Supply organizations change their techniques to cook their office items for individuals that need at-home usefulness, similar to solace and accommodation.

- **Scientific:**

An innovative business climate incorporates the improvement of new innovation, how individuals collaborate with innovation, and its natural impacts. Advancement can affect an affiliation's inner and outside conditions. On the inside, it might have an effect on things like the cost of production or how to automate particular tasks. Remotely, innovation can influence how shoppers speak with one another and how rapidly they adjust to progressions in the field.

An illustration of the technological business environment is the provision of automated solutions by technology companies for the construction of components for larger machinery, thereby reducing the need for human labor. Organizations that produce merchandise change their inner techniques to focus on amplifying efficiency by using the aptitude of laborers. Moreover, the resistance uses new web-based business development to simplify buying things, which makes one association need to use a comparable advancement.

* **Suppliers:**

Providers' surroundings include elements that could impact your providers' presentation, which can then influence your business. The costs of producing goods, the availability of resources, and employees' dependability are all possible components of this environment. The amount of time your company needs to focus on production and adjust to changes like price and availability can be determined by understanding the environment of your suppliers. Different conditions, such as political and monetary conditions, can likewise influence a provider's current circumstance.

- **Concurrence:**

A serious climate is the means by which organizations inside your market change and capability and what this could mean for your business. This can incorporate when different kinds of contenders, both bigger and more modest than your organization, could enter or leave the market, as this could influence various ways of behaving like brand situating. Financial and market conditions frequently influence cutthroat conditions as organizations could change their procedures, empowering you to do likewise.

- **Political:**

A political business climate can include exercises in states or other lawful bodies that impact how organizations could work. This business climate is impacted by different variables, including new guidelines, approaches from organizations, and the steadiness of the public authority. If new investment policies or new import and export regulations are implemented, this environment may alter other factors, such as the environment of suppliers.

An illustration of the political and business climate is a manufacturing company that makes steel equipment for aerospace companies. Production may also be delayed if trade negotiations with the nation that provides the majority of their materials are delayed. Import taxes are increased by the government, driving up the cost of steel imports. The assembling organization looks for nearby steel suppliers to stay away from delays and diminish costs, adjusting to these natural changes.

- **Genuine:**

A characteristic business climate is the means by which actual areas, similar to geology and environment, can influence organizations. Disasters caused by the weather, the availability of natural resources, and conservation are all potential influences on this. Frequently, regular habitats converge with others, as in the world of politics. For instance, the government has enacted new laws to protect the environment that restrict the number of raw goods you can receive.

- **Inside:**

Inward business conditions incorporate variables like arrangements, organization culture, and business execution. Organizations oftentimes have control over their inward surroundings rather than numerous other outside business conditions. This can incorporate redesigning jobs and business structures or advancing exercises that match the organization culture. You could change interior strategies assuming that your current circumstance has high representative turnover or lower efficiency.

WHY IS A BUSINESS CLIMATE VITAL TO GET?

Understanding business conditions has different basic advantages, including:

- **Seeing movements:**

Understanding the various conditions assists you with figuring out changes that influence the market and how you could reply. You can sort out how each environment affects others and how you could prepare for with a more significant cognizance of these changes.

- **Distinguishing potential open doors:**

Climate mindfulness can assist you with recognizing open doors where you could work within your control and distinguish patterns. For instance, changes in a world of politics that could confine imports could provoke you to investigate neighborhood chances to keep up with creation levels.

- **Building notoriety:**

Answering different business conditions can show shoppers you're mindful of different elements on the planet. Understanding your clients' societies and creating delicate substances or items that allure them can assist you with building your standing in sociocultural conditions.

CHAPTER 3

THE INFLUENTIAL ABILITY

The capacity to impact and organize individuals from cross-utilitarian groups at different levels, including peers, upper administration, and direct reports, is essential. When it comes to managing cross-practical groups, the circumstance becomes precarious as there is no immediate, various-level impact that one can apply to individuals in different groups.

When people are a part of a project team, cross-functional workgroup, or task force, it is frequently necessary to use influence or persuasion to get things done and accomplish the goals.

There is a need to persuade and convince people across layers and social events to accomplish individual and different, evened-out targets. In this situation, one can't underrate the job of 'impacting abilities.'

The ability to "sell" an idea to key stakeholders in the various teams both internally and externally within the client organizations is essential for success in the current position. One might think of a splendid thought or an answer; however, the acknowledgment of the thought for execution can frequently present difficulties, except if one cuts out an arrangement to 'impact' key partners.

I would say that I have understood that this can frequently be a drawn- out process and may require a very long time before the thought can see the following stages towards execution.

At the point when individuals are put under an excess of tension, it can frequently hurt their inner selves and lead to undesirable contentions.

The unfortunate results should be visible due to methods of postponement, time and cost overloads, and inadequate execution. Pressure or force, as it is sometimes referred to, can frequently result in "win-lose scenarios," which can cause dissatisfaction among the parties involved—individuals or teams—and eventually result in a loss of goodwill and negative relationships.

Finding a way to become "inclusive" means being able to motivate others to achieve significant goals in a way that benefits everyone (individuals, internal and external teams, if they are involved). Only when parties involved bring their "influencing skills" to the forefront can an overall "win-win" feeling be created. The foundation upon which goals can be accomplished and outcomes sustained over time is the capacity to influence others.

Nowadays, employees are under pressure to accomplish more with fewer resources. It is generally important to act rapidly and translate activities into results. One requirement is to team up through the force of impacting and influence to compensate for absence of information and abilities in various regions and look for commitment from others. Groups can now work from anywhere because of innovation, and it's basic to utilize the worldwide ability pool and capacities to accomplish objectives. While this is a reality, it is vital to take note of that impacting and influence can assume a key part in uniting different groups for in general achievement.

It is central to foster associations with the specialty of influencing. The course of impact ignited areas of strength. In the art of influencing, one important part is to build credibility. To have impact, one should be seen as being valid and reliable. ' The quotient of self-orientation needs to be low, indicating that one is working for the benefit of the organization as a whole and disregarding one's own desires.

The capacity to impact and facilitate with individuals from cross-practical groups at different levels, including peers, upper administration, and direct reports, is essential. When it comes to managing cross-practical groups, the circumstance becomes precarious as there is no immediate, various-level impact that one can apply to individuals in different groups.

When people are a part of a project team, cross-functional workgroup, or task force, it is frequently necessary to use influence or persuasion to get things done and accomplish the goals.

There is a need to persuade and convince people across layers and social events to accomplish individual and different, evened-out targets. In this arising situation, one can't underrate the job of 'impacting abilities.'

The ability to "sell" an idea to key stakeholders in the various teams both internally and externally within the client organizations is essential for success in the current position.

One might think of a splendid thought or an answer; however, the acknowledgment of the thought for execution can frequently present difficulties, except if one cuts out an arrangcmcnt to 'impact' key partners. I would say that I have understood that this can frequently be a drawn-out process and may require a very long time before the thought can see the following stages towards execution.

There is a need to persuade and convince people across layers and social events to accomplish individual and different evened-out targets. The unfortunate results should be visible in the methods of postponements, time and cost overloads, and inadequate execution. Pressure or force, as it is sometimes referred to, can frequently result in "win-lose scenarios," which can cause dissatisfaction among the parties involved—individuals or teams—and eventually result in a loss of goodwill and negative relationships.

Finding a way to become "inclusive" means being able to motivate others to achieve significant goals in a way that benefits everyone (individuals, internal and external teams, if they are involved). Only when parties involved bring their "influencing skills" to the forefront can an overall "win-win" feeling be created. The foundation upon which goals can be accomplished and outcomes sustained over time is the capacity to influence others.

Nowadays, employees are under pressure to accomplish more with fewer resources. It is generally important to act rapidly and make an interpretation of activities into results. One requirement is to team up through the force of impact and influence to compensate for the absence of information and abilities in various regions and look for commitment from others. Groups can now work from anywhere on account of innovation, and it's basic to utilize the worldwide ability pool and capacities to accomplish objectives. While this is a reality, it is vital to take note that impact and influence can play a key role in uniting different groups for general achievement.

It is central to foster associations with the specialty of influencing. The course of impact starts with areas of strength. In the art of influencing, one important part is to build credibility. To have impact, one should be seen as being valid and reliable. ' The quotient of self-orientation needs to be low, indicating that one is working for the benefit of the organization as a whole and disregarding one's own desires.

CHAPTER 4

TOOLS AND TECHNIQUES FOR ACHIEVING SALES GOALS

What are sales goals?

Deal objectives are benchmarks that individuals from an association set to keep tabs on their development and guarantee that their business develops and stays beneficial. In order to evaluate a company's quality, efficiency, or marketing success, as well as their impact on sales and revenue, they may concentrate on a specific metric or key performance indicator (KPI). There are different deals objectives an organization can set to work on, generally speaking, to benefit and oversee efficiency, including:

1. Support the worth of your typical deal:
Without increasing the number of sales or the amount of time spent developing additional leads, you can boost your profit and revenue by increasing the value of your average sales. Consider adding an extra component or decision to your client proposals to upgrade your arrangements.

2. Keep an eye on your sales efforts:
Consider continuously measuring a few specific metrics or key performance indicators to monitor your sales activities. This can assist you with sorting out which practices assist you in arriving at your business objective and which regions could utilize some work.

3. Diminish the length of the business interaction to a minimum:

Assuming that your deal interaction is long and confounded, you could experience difficulty arriving at your objectives. To assist you with arriving at your objectives, contemplate shortening them. Prior to talking with a deal prospect, you might want to think about creating a concise three-point agenda to make sure you stay focused and concise.

4. Boost your conversion rate:

In the event that you work at your local rate, you might require less leads and can invest more energy sustaining effective arrangements and further developing client assistance and fulfillment. Consider adjusting your pitch to feature the worth of your item and how it can address your imminent client's needs or concerns.

5. Look for references from past clients:

By contributing nothing to your effort and using informal exchange advertising, client references can assist you in setting aside time and cash. They can help you with additional brand care among your vested parties, so consider mentioning references to help with achieving your arrangement targets.

6. Overcome client resistance:

You may be able to overcome any of the client's initial reluctance or hesitancy by being persistent, which can be an essential component of lead nurturing. On the off chance that the client isn't keen on the arrangement right now, you should make a note in your schedule to reach out to them in the following quarter.

7. Network with individuals who might give extra leads:

Utilizing your contacts and networking with people who may provide additional leads and clients is one strategy for increasing sales and achieving your objectives. Consider exploring your web-based entertainment stages and auditing who might interface with likely possibilities to track down new expected clients.

8. Meet with a little gathering of partners or confided-in companions:

You might profit from getting criticism and backing from other similar experts, so think about gathering with a small gathering of partners or confided in companions. Visiting with others can help you with investigating your progression and planning your direction, and it may help keep you liable in the meantime.

9. Make action goals:

Outreach activities that aim to encourage the completion of sales-related tasks like emails, phone calls, and appointments may be included in one aspect of your plan. This can assist you in determining the activities that result in the highest rate of lead generation or deal closure, in addition to tracking sales.

10. Before setting new goals, review your weekly progress:

Looking into your week-by-week execution can permit you to pursue informed choices prior to laying out objectives for the impending week. You can look back at what went well and figure out parts of your strategy that could use some work.

11. Assign time to prospects:

Prospecting can be a significant part of meeting your deals objectives, so consider devoting a particular timeframe consistently to looking for clients who might be keen on your item. It might help you to plainly comprehend the people who can profit from your association's labor and products so you can engage them straightforwardly.

12. Cover your channel still:

You might want to keep a close eye on it to see if you can direct your sweats and increase deals If your channel starts to get low. You can figure out where to concentrate your sweats to stay on track and achieve your pretensions by assessing your channel.

13. Conduct progress reviews each quarter:

For each quintet, suppose that making a list of three main precedents that your platoon can use to concentrate on and direct their lower deals pretensions. This can guarantee that all individualities add to analogous generally speaking results and have a common attention.

14. Enhance your styles of client service:

Fastening on consumer fidelity can help an association with working on its standing inside its assiduity, so further developing customer care might help guests with passing through your business and stay faithful to the association.

guests may partake in their gests with other implicit guests, which can boost deals.

15. Set   objects grounded on data and objective information:

Rather than a director's opinion or preferences to   insure that a   platoon can achieve its deal pretensions. Use data to help make setting deal presumptions less stressful. Statistical surveying can likewise illuminate deal reps about guests' inclinations and   requirements, which is data they might use while meeting with a possibility.

16. Educate and inform members of the deals platoon:

An association might benefit from considering its outreach group individuals' means, failings, and technical motifs before settling on their new targets. Organizations that commit time to worker's expert advancement can help with staffing   individualities, work on   their donations, and show them they are a resource for the group.

17. **Frame and   concentrate on your objects:**

Together with the members of your platoon, prioritize the objects in order of significance and outgrowth, focusing on the objects that give the association the most value. This may help the platoon as a whole complete tasks and achieve milestones together.

18. **Asking open- concluded questions can help you learn more still:**

You might want to consider asking them open-concluded questions when you talk to them If you want to learn   further about a implicit client's precedences and values. This can permit you to find your way to deal with their particular prerequisites, which might help you with settling the concession.

19. Take good care of yourself:

It does not count how big or small the business deal is, it's important to take care of your health and get enough rest and relaxation. Feeling good and refreshed can help you with keeping up with your energy and center while meeting with possibilities or making bargains.

20.Suppose about setting lower pretensions still:

You might want to break them down into lower ones that professionals might be more comfortable achieving, If you or your platoon members find it delicate to achieve large deals pretensions. This can help with structure representative certainty and confidence, which might help them with moving toward manages an agitated standpoint.

21. Center around critical thinking instead of a specific item. While experts might attempt to pitch particulars to guests in view of their inclinations and requirements, they might have further accomplishment by resolving a customer's concern and aiding them with fostering an answer. Probative conversations can show a customer that your association thinks frequently about their interests and makes creative answers for them.

22. Give yourself and other people a price for their sweats It may be discouraging if

you don't close a deal or if your platoon fails to meet their daily pretensions. As opposed to belaboring on these occasions, award yourself and your mates for their capacities and trials, and remain certain about new likely guests or in- progress leads.

23. Work on the acceptability of design leads' methodologies   Deals directors and trainers have the capability to guide and support the strategies and sweats of their brigades, so enhancing directors' styles may be salutary to the association as a whole. In order to comprehend the conditions or enterprises of the salesmen, a   director of deals can invite feedback and collaboration.

24. Make use of online selling Virtual selling strategies can be used by an association to

reach a wider range of implicit guests if they're applicable to the business and its members. This can help deal with joining dwindle trip time and commit further energy to getting ready for arrangements and supporting leads.

25. Engage in active listening with concentrated attention can help you find out about the customer's needs or wants. Avoiding interruptions and paying attention to the speakers' body language, verbal communication, and words are all part of this strategy.

26. Concentrate on the timeline of your customer While it veritably well might be solicitous to zero in on your deals arrestment times, focusing on your customer's course of events can help you make a significant association and show

them that you care about their requirements. This might help you with settling a concession and work on the customer's sapience.

27. Consider your unique selling point. Check what compels your employer to the same as its rivals. You can connect with conceivable outcomes and conclude your association's worth by rehearsing this momentous perspective.

28. Try not to bandy contenders As opposed to talking negatively about your rivals, ask the purchaser inquiries about their interests or values that feature how your item or association can accommodate their conjurations better than different associations in the business. This can assist you in chipping away at your

remaining without discussing your adversaries.

29. Dockets and asked-for issues should be communicated All an outreach group might profit when its individuals comprehend their targets and how they connect with a further noteworthy ideal or result. Dockets can help an association keep its members informed and on the same design.

30. Use account operation to maintain connections with guests. The board can help you guarantee customer fulfillment and keep lines of correspondence open between your employer and its guests. By maintaining or perfecting client retention, this can help you in adding profit.

31. Show your appreciation by making it a top priority to thank your guests for their uninterrupted support and business. E-mails or thank- you cards can easily leave a lasting impression on a client and encourage them to stay pious.

32. Suppose about the platoon's advantages Feting the   platoon's strengths and employing the styles and strategies that enable them to exceed can be salutary to an association. People can express what helps them succeed and how to cultivate these strategies through communication across the deals platoon.

33. Maintain   thoughtlessness   Being thoughtful can demonstrate to implicit guests that you're interested in addressing their preferences and resolving their issues. This can make your business more

significant to the outreach group and possible guests.

34. Do what inspires and motivates you

Having some good times and getting a charge out of what you really do can help you with meeting each arrangement with energy and alleviation. This may demonstrate to the customer that you truly watch about them and their requirements or precedences, as well as help you enjoy your profession.

35. Establish pretensions for the coming time

Each time, an association can have a gathering of its business representatives to examine their advancement and set new targets for the impending time. Experts might consider the general drives that can help the association and how to carry out them ahead long.

36. Every day, review your pretensions
Before you start handling your tasks and liabilities, you might want to suppose about reviewing your deals pretensions each day. Staying focused and setting precedences for your day can be made easier with this.

CHAPTER 5

TURNING DIFFICULTIES INTO OPEN DOORS

Obstacles are a necessary component of life. Whether it be testing times, individuals or conditions - the majority of us can connect with facing barricades in life that vibe hard, unreasonable, or in any event, destroying now and again.

Certain individuals face the most unbelievable misfortunes and some way or another come out the opposite side more grounded. Others disintegrate under the heaviness of the pressure and enduring they are encountering. A similar test and situation one individual could ascend from, could become another person's long lasting wretchedness they won't ever recuperate from.

Strength is an asset that seems to change troubles into open entryways for improvement during bothering times.

The inquiry then becomes: How can we avoid becoming ensnared or swallowed up by our challenges and instead grow from them? How would we arrange that transition to assist us go forward rather than hold us back?

Although there is no easy or "one-size-fits-all" way to become more resilient, the following suggestions can assist in transforming challenges into opportunities for self-transformation and business expansion:

- **Point of view:**

The focal point we view our reality through is however individual as we may be. What we see and accept to be valid isn't reality; it is "our" truth. If the truth we live by no longer serves us or forces us to repeatedly learn the same difficult lesson, it might be time to consider adopting a new perspective that "will" move us forward.

A very liberating and enlightening experience might result from changing our point of view.

Various methodologies can be embraced to determine a near-term issue and make new choices. As a matter of fact, this change might help us take on a new, blissful point of view.

Compassion for others and for ourselves becomes more natural when we practice looking at life and business from different perspectives. With viewpoint, we can draw closer to tracking down the illustration or a chance for development in pretty much any circumstance.

- **Trustworthiness:**

We must be open with ourselves if we are to move forward.

What do we truly think often about?

What are our needs? How are we truly feeling?

We can give the impression to those around us that everything is great by putting on a brave face or sugarcoating the situation. In any case, as a matter of fact, a serious feeling of disquiet will before long start to crawl into our being.

We could possibly trick ourselves for some time into trusting the veneer, yet we will not have the option to stow away from who we truly are for extremely lengthy.

The sooner we are straightforward with ourselves, our organizations and honor ourselves by residing from a position of individual truth - the simpler it becomes to confront moves with elegance and a readiness to learn.

We will feel more at peace the more closely we align the image we project into the world with our inner truth. We will experience unwavering inner strength only when we speak and act in accordance with our truth. Having areas of strength for a with ourselves doesn't eliminate difficulties, yet it assists us with traveling through each phase of a test with greater ease.

- **Openness:**

At the point when we approach life and business space prepared, open and ready to push ahead- that's precisely exact thing we will do. The fellow is valid for when we're cut off and decline to move on an issue that causes us pressure- we will remain stayed with a analogous degree of intensity. At the point when we allow ourselves to open up to the chance of" unsticking" ourselves and pushing ahead the world responds by opening dependent upon us. In some cases being available to fresh openings and perspectives requires a monster act of pure trust. It   constantly implies we're pushing past our usual ranges of familiarity. This can be veritably awkward. Whenever we really do take that threat and have kindly further confidence all the while, we're compensated through the factual change. Life is an astonishing excursion and we get to pick anyhow of whether we witness it fully- the hard aspects what not. In the event that we can incline toward the torture with a touch of fresh plumpness and receptiveness to the literacy, the exemplifications extend in the most lovely way. We can help with changing our difficulties into open doors for development by permitting the battles to extend. By moving" through" the snags, rather than stowing down from them. likewise, by encountering each and every piece of the excursion, without losing ourselves en route. All through the excursion of life, we're managed the cost of chances to develop and extend our extent of what is conceivable   constantly. We're encircled by similar   innumerous mind boggling   effects, individualities and business   occasion. We're more likely to find the   provocation to move forward, live completely, break further ground, reach   further   implicit   guests,   grow exponentially, and heal great injuries if we're open and curious.

- **Connect with winners:**

Your companions are like lifts they either bring you up, or cut you down." What you   conjure about and what you encounter are told by the people you hang out with. What is further, the impacts and the fantasies lead to your changes. By altering your circle, you can alter the outgrowth." Just make sure you truly   watch about these people and are not just using them to advance yourself. individualities are strikingly great at tracking down a phony.

* **Consider yourself fortunate:**

They also follow up on surprising open doors and association well with others since they are interested, while unfortunate individualities will more frequently than not be tense and pass up on open doors. This appears to be legal considering specialists have set up daring people ameliorate in business and life since they do not avoid difficulties or implicit open doors that might startle.

* **Show kindness:**

Consider the misers you know. Is it safe to say that they are your #1 individuals? Wharton teacher and creator Adam Award says individuals will applaud and root you when you pick the provider approach. Unquestionably your opportunities for progress are more noteworthy with additional individuals in your corner.

- **Be interested**:

How much do you truly have some familiarity with individuals you perhaps look out for a way to improve against, whether it's your colleagues, the café barista who makes your latte consistently or even individuals you've known perpetually yet might be underestimating.

- **Start posing more inquiries:**

No one can tell what you'll find or where you'll take your newly discovered information.

- **Be perfectly positioned:**

Try meeting individuals who work in your organization's space or have business sharpness you can gain from. This could include going to industry occasions, neighborhood meetups or the numerous gatherings Inc. puts on over time, for business pioneers forcefully seeking after development.

- **Post insightful discourse on the web:**

Invest some energy at high-traffic sites connected with your industry or ability and contribute smart remarks to their gatherings. This is an effective method for setting up a good foundation for yourself as a specialist as well as a chance to pass on a connection to your site or blog. What might this at some point get you? More connections and social media followers who might invite you to speak at an event or serve as a source for an interview with the media.

- **Recognize the bias toward attractiveness:**

You can check this two different ways out.

To begin with, really try to introduce yourself as spotless and sharp looking. You can show improvement over the latest thing of wearing athletic wear, for example, yoga pants in almost any setting. Furthermore, assuming halitosis or stench are an issue, have a go at changing your microbiome-the microorganisms that live in and on your body. Notwithstanding oral enhancements that give valuable microscopic organisms that will battle against smell causing microorganisms, you'll get sound probiotics from matured food sources, for example, kefir, sauerkraut, kimchi and fermented tea, all of which you can find in your neighborhood wellbeing food sources store.

All the more significantly, however, don't remove yourself from individuals you judge to be not exactly appealing. Everybody, no matter what their shell, has a story to tell. Also, it very well may be one you really want to hear.

CHAPTER 6

CONCLUSION OF THE NEGOTIATIONS

(How do you fix the deal?)

What exactly is a negotiation?

Negotiation is an exchange where at least two sides cooperate to arrive at a pleasant answer for all. It could lead to a formal agreement like a contract or a verbal agreement like a contract.

In the event that you realize how trades work and what abilities are required, you could possibly find a decent solution.

Negotiation is a conversation to resolve questions and reach an agreement between at least two sides.

Negotiation is a "compromise" process that brings about a trade-off where each side makes a concession to support all interested parties.

There are numerous circumstances where you might be a moderator. You may be engaged in arranging a proposition for employment, requesting a raise, revitalizing for a financial plan increment, trading property, or bringing a deal to a close with a client. To find success with any of them, you should have the option to arrange

Huge Abilities for Discussion

The following are a few key exchange abilities that might be useful in your profession:

1. Communication:

Fundamental relational abilities incorporate recognizing nonverbal prompts and verbal abilities to effectively communicate your thoughts. Skilled negotiators are able to adapt their communication styles to the requirements of the listener. By laying out clear correspondence, you can keep away from false impressions that could keep you from arriving at a split decision.

2. Undivided attention:

Undivided attention abilities are likewise urgent for grasping someone else's perspective in discussion. Dissimilar to uninvolved tuning in, which is hearing a speaker without holding their message, undivided attention guarantees you draw in and later review explicit subtleties without requiring data to be rehashed.

3. The capacity to appreciate anyone on a profound level:

The capacity to control one's emotions and recognize the feelings of others is called emotional intelligence. During a negotiation, being aware of the emotional dynamics can help you remain calm and focused on the main issues. On the off chance that you're unsatisfied with the ongoing discussion, request a break so you and the other party can get back with invigorated points of view.

4. Tolerance:

Many changes can take a large chuck of the day to finish, periodically including renegotiation and counteroffers. In order to duly assess a situation and arrive at the stylish decision for their guests, mediators constantly demonstrate tolerance rather than seeking a quick resolution.

5. Rigidity:

Inflexibility is necessary for fruitful discussion. The circumstances may alter from day to day because every concession is unique. An involved party might, for example, suddenly alter their demands. While it's trying to anticipate what's passing, a decent prolocutor can acclimate fleetingly and decide on another arrangement if necessary.

6. Persuasion:

An important skill in accommodations is being able to impact other people. It can help you characterize why your proposed arrangement helps all gatherings and prompt others to help you share your perspective. Mediators should be assertive when necessary in addition to being dominant . Resoluteness permits you to offer your shoes while regarding the contrary side's points of view.

7. Problem- working:

To identify a problem and find a result in concession, problem- working chops are needed. In the event that a cost is exorbitantly high, how might it be brought down? Chancing exceptional answers for issues might be the deciding element in split the difference. How can be compensated for the absence of an asset?

8. Decision- making:

During a concession, good mediators can make quick opinions. During a concession, it may be necessary to agree to a concession. You should have the option to conclusively respond. Flash back that your choices might lastingly affect yourself or your association. It's vital to completely consider your choices cautiously without overthinking your choice. Interspersing between your choices without an unmistakable response could bring meaningless pressure.

9. Comity structure The capacity to construct affinity allows you to lay out associations with others where the two sides feel upheld and comprehended. Understanding the other person's wants and needs and communicating your pretensions are necessary for developing fellowship. Affinity helps ease pressures, advances common trouble and improves the probability of agreeing. To fabricate comity, extending appreciation and exercising concentrated attention capacities are introductory.

10. Planning Exchange expects intending to help you with figuring out what you need and how the terms will be satisfied. You should suppose about the stylish outgrowth, the least respectable offer, and what you'll do if you cannot come to an agreement. Preparing, getting ready are imperative to a productive trade. The stylish intercessors enter a discussion with commodities like one fall back, yet all the same, constantly more. Suppose about every single imaginable result and be ready for every one of these situations. For mediators, this is the" stylish volition to a negotiated agreement"(BATNA).

11. Integrity Respectability, or having solid morals and moral norms, is an abecedarian moxie for addresses. The

other side can trust what you say if you're thoughtful, regardful, and honest. You should be suitable to keep the pledges you make as a moderator. Avoid over-promising in order to establish credibility.

12. Assumption the directors also as you ought to enter a discussion with a reasonable ideal, the contrary side, likewise, has its own characterized hypotheticals. On the off chance that you accept, you presumably will not have the option to assent to one another's terms. You could take a stab at changing your hypotheticals. Maintaining a balance between being an establishment moderator and a cooperative one is necessary for professed anticipation operations.

SUCCESSFUL NEGOTIATION TIPS

Consider the following in order to better prepare for negotiations:

1. Do your homework:

Prior to going into exchange talks, assess all sides and think about their objectives. It can likewise be useful to investigate the individual you are haggling with. Figure out the limits of the arbitrator. Might you at any point get what you want from them? Having an address comprehension of these roadblocks can assist you with arrangement.

2. Know what you value most:

Dealings frequently require each side to think twice about. Realize what is generally vital to you and what you are prepared to forfeit for.

Laying out your boundaries early can assist you in assessing what you won't surrender and where you're willing to move. Be clear about what each side offers and what they need from each other if you are the negotiator.

3. Think about the resistance:

Consider the opposition to your negotiations that might arise. Do you believe that declining sales will cause your manager to oppose a pay raise? Will you be denied a higher beginning compensation for a position in light of the fact that your mentioned rate is over the normal range? Record every one of the likely resistances, and afterward accumulate the data you can use to contend with your situation.

4. Keep correspondences open:

To lessen the likelihood of confusion, present your objectives, goals, and expectations consistently. Utilize your verbal and nonverbal social capacities, as well as your non-verbal correspondence. Take a stab at commonly valuable arrangements; however, be ready to think twice about them.

Assuming you are the mediator, guarantee there are rules for the conversation and that the two sides stick to them. Make a hard copy of arrangements.

5. Decide when to depart:

One of the hardest parts of negotiating is knowing when to give up. Before beginning any discussions, it is essential to foresee differences.

It's probably time to end the talks once you realize that terms cannot be agreed upon and that further concessions cannot be made.

6. Keep in mind your timetable:

A course of events can essentially influence your place in the exchange. In the event that one or the two sides are hurrying to arrive at a choice, one might surrender excessively and lament their activities. For instance, in the event that you're attempting to find another line of work rapidly, you might take a situation with lower pay or compromise a lot on benefits. In this situation, you might find yourself unsatisfied with your choice over the long haul.

EFFECTIVE DISCUSSION TECHNIQUES

You've mastered the fundamentals of good discussion procedures: You do a thorough job of preparation, spend time establishing rapport, make your first offer once you have a clear idea of your bargaining range, and look for smart tradeoffs across issues to create value. Presently, now is the ideal time to retain five less popular yet also viable discussion subjects and procedures that can help every expert mediator:

1. Reevaluate nervousness as energy:
Unpleasant side effects, such as sweaty palms, a racing heart, and an overwhelming sense of anxiety, frequently occur during the preparation phase of a negotiation. Even professional negotiators experience anxiety from time to time, but this state of mind can cause us to make costly choices.

We frequently believe that the best way to manage our anxiety during discussions is to cool down, yet doing so can be challenging.

Try recasting anxiety's high physiological arousal as excitement.

Improve your ability to negotiate effectively and become a better dealmaker and leader

2. A draft agreement serves as the focus of the discussion:

The anchoring bias, first discovered by psychologists Amos Tversky and Daniel Kahneman, states that the person who makes the first offer in a negotiation is more likely to influence the discussion in her favor. Even for professional negotiators with a lot of experience, first offers often act as strong anchors. To have a much greater effect, you could take a stab at opening meaningful talks with a draft understanding, or standard-structure contract, ready with your legitimate guidance and any important leaders from your group. However such drafts aren't generally proper, they can expand your impact over the exchange, as per Tufts College teacher Jeswald Salacuse. A standard-structure contract not just purposes the securing predisposition for your potential benefit yet could save the two sides time and cash, making this one of the exchange methods that could truly merit attempting.

3. Take advantage of silence's power:

In exchange, as in any conversation, we will generally rush in to fill any awkward hushes that emerge with influence strategies and counter-contentions. Allowing a few moments of silence after your partner speaks can give you time to fully process what he said. Quietness enable you to hose your senses for self-support and enhance your impulse to tune in," as per Subramanian. Quietness can likewise assist you with stopping your own inclination toward the securing predisposition. Subramanian asserts that "your stunned silence will far more effectively defuse the anchor than heaps of protesting would" in the event that a counterpart fires an outrageous anchor.

4. Ask for help:

Proficient arbitrators frequently accept that asking the other party for exhortation will convey shortcoming, freshness, or both.

According to some psychologists, when we ask someone for help, we congratulate them and increase their self-confidence.

Thus, consider making a move to ask your partner for counsel when you genuinely need it. In addition to the fact that you are probably going to profit from the counsel, however, you might reinforce the relationship all the while.

5. Put a fair proposal under a magnifying glass with conclusive proposition discretion:

While haggling to end a debate under the shadow of a claim, you could end up disappointed by a partner's appearing powerlessness to make or engage sensible, pure intentions. In such a hostile negotiation, how can you reach a settlement that is fair for both parties? Final-offer arbitration (FOA), commonly referred to as baseball arbitration, is a potential but underutilised instrument, according to Max H. Bazerman, a professor at Harvard Business School.

In FOA, each party makes its best and final offer to an arbitrator, who has to choose between two offers and no other value.

Neither side shall be permitted to appeal the arbitrator's ruling.

At the point when gatherings consent to utilize FOA, their offers normally become sensible, as they currently have a motivator to intrigue the mediator with their sensibility. In Major League Baseball, where FOA is available, players and teams typically reach an agreement on contract disputes because they are concerned about what an arbitrator might decide. Whenever you are in a question with somebody you accept is being preposterous, consider proposing FOA, suggests Bazerman. She will likely respond to your suggestion with a much more reasonable offer if she has been bluffing.

You ought to be positive about your capacity to persuade the mediator that your deal is sensible assuming she acknowledges it.

CHAPTER 7

SCALING YOUR BUSINESS

Building a fruitful organization is about significantly more than expanding deals and income.

When scaling a business, an organisation needs the appropriate strategy, staff, and procedures to support new clients, goods, and services.

While any business chief fantasizes about turning into an unexpected phenomenon, fruitful scaling includes building and executing a long term, practical procedure. Regardless of the size of your business, understanding scaling and recognizing noteworthy advances you can take to do both are key to arriving at your objectives.

What does "scaling a business" mean?

The expressions "development" and "scale" are frequently utilized reciprocally. While the two are connected, they have unmistakable contrasts. Development happens when an organization's income increments at similar rate as its consumption of new assets, like cash, innovation, or workers.

Then again, scaling is the point at which an association distinguishes ways of developing all the more effectively, bringing about income development at a considerably more noteworthy rate than expansions in assets and costs.

Planning strategically and with care is essential for growing a business.

Normal errors organizations frequently make during the scaling system include:

- Scaling too quickly

- Putting short-term goals ahead of long-term objectives
- Losing focus
- Hiring for quantity rather than quality
- Disregard for cycles and frameworks in order to increase productivity
- Lacking agility

Businesses that scale successfully take into account how the process affects all aspects of the organization.

Key components include:

- **Organization objectives:**

It's important to focus on both short-term and long-term goals when setting goals to grow your business.

By putting an unnecessary accent on momentary objectives, your association risks developing excessively fast and disregarding the infrastructural needs for long-term achievement. When planning your scaling strategy, keep in mind both the process goals and the outcome goals.

By putting an unjustifiable accent on momentary objectives, your association risks developing excessively fast and discarding the foundation prerequisites for long- haul achievement. For instance, on the off chance that your result objective is to twofold your client degree of consistency, recognize noteworthy advances you will take to further develop the client experience and commitment. In order for your team to be ready to pivot your strategy if the market or customer needs change, remaining agile is another important aspect of goal setting.

- **Number of colleagues:**

Organizations that scale excessively fast could make the presumption that assuming the objective is to twofold income, this implies the association likewise needs to twofold headcount. This isn't probably going to be an economical procedure, particularly in the event that income development eases back. Quality should come first when building your team, not quantity. Hire competent leaders who are able to supervise and inspire team members. Hire talented people who have the specialized skills you need to achieve your business objectives.

- **Inward cycles:**

Implementing effective standardized workflows and repeatable day-to-day procedures is crucial to business growth. Think about which processes—such as onboarding team members, invoicing customers, or requesting a marketing asset—can be automated or made more efficient to help your business scale more effectively.

It is not scalable to have team members create their own processes each time they complete a task or implement a strategy.

It takes longer to manually complete work and makes it harder for new team members to get up to speed.

Having procedures in place and documented can considerably increase your company's capacity to grow.

How to expand your company.

At the point when you grow a business, you add clients and colleagues while costs likewise increment. At the end of the day, your business is filling in size however not income, which isn't practical, particularly on the off chance that you experience a plunge in customer base. If this happens, you'll only have resources and employees, but no work or money to support them.

At the point when you scale your business, you add assets and colleagues as income develops however at a more slow rate than the development of your client list. Therefore, your business scales in a reasonable way, permitting edges to increment gradually over the long haul. Furthermore, in the event that you experience a dunk in customer base, your income is sufficiently still to support your labor force and asset costs.

LEARNING HOW TO SCALE A BUSINESS

What steps do you take to grow a company? To make a functioning definition, you should consider starting and grow a business.

You began your organization to fulfill a market need, bring in cash, and maybe even satisfy a fantasy. Business extension is significant if you have any desire to proceed to benefit and grow your market.

Business expansion is frequently referred to as "hockey stick growth," in which a company experiences explosive revenue growth following a period of linear expansion. Fast development is charming, however zeroing in on this immediately can make a few business visionaries lose center. Exclusive focus like this reduces the significance of the straight development time frame that precedes the rising handle of the hockey stick - the sharp edge - where the most basic work is finished over, ordinarily, three to four years.

Utilizing this "blade period" to implement systems and procedures for long-term, profitable growth is necessary for scaling a business. What's more, the cutting edge period is where you lay out your basic beliefs, organization culture, and brand character, foster the client experience, and make your underlying plan of action. To put it plainly, it's the represent the deciding moment time of any business.

It is trying to Scale a business; It necessitates a methodical approach as well as a solid foundation for when you encounter a rapid growth curve. When considering mindfully scaling a business, the following should be kept in mind:

STEERS FOR HOW TO RESULT A BUSINESS

We're implying improvement strategies that assist your business method while watching out for the impact of headway on your relationship as we with examining how to scale a business.

A dependable and long-lasting strategy for scaling a business can be found in the following pointers.

1. Know your Motivation:

Scaling a business depends on making client steadfastness, and zeroing in on worker unwaveringly is the most effective way to construct client devotion. At the point when your workers are cheerful, they'll get the news out and pass on their excitement for your organization. Representatives are steadfast when their motivation and values line up with their organization, and they feel their professions have a higher reason.

In the event that you don't begin with your "why" of starting a new business in any case, then figuring out how to scale a business is of restricted utility. The best way to make your employees raving fans of your business and naturally drive growth is to have a clear understanding of your purpose and effectively communicate it to your team.

2. Building a business map:

The majority of business owners have a business plan, but have you considered creating a business map?

A convincing and comprehensive technique for growing a business and achieving its goals is a business map.

It additionally prompts you to ask fundamental inquiries like "what business would you say you are truly ready?" also "for what reason did you get into this business in any case?"

Business maps rouse you to contemplate where you've been, the explanation you started your association, and where you really want to go. For example, what comes next for your company, and where does it ultimately go in an ideal world?

Reporting these objectives is a significant piece of figuring out how to scale a business and will be a useful reference when challenges go crazy.

3. Amazing your Item or Administration:

While zeroing in on monstrous development, numerous entrepreneurs neglect to guarantee that they offer a strong item or administration, frequently calculating that they'll fix the issue subsequent to getting more clients or dispersion.

Be that as it may, in the event that you don't dispose of the bugs first, they'll deteriorate while scaling a business. Figuring out how to scale a business prior to seeking after development will set aside you cerebral pains and cash over the long haul.

As your association creates, it's fundamental to zero in on buyer input, spot issues, and work on your recommendations until they fulfill their expectations.

Many issues with growth will disappear when you produce a high-quality product or service. Because you will have a deeper comprehension of what you and your customers want and need from your product or service, addressing first-iteration issues also helps you assume control when scaling your business.

4. Create well-thought-out processes and procedures:

Scaling a business requires more than just expanding upward and outward. It likewise includes guaranteeing that your inward cycles in general and tasks do effortlessly.

The last thing you want is to lose clients you've endeavored to get as a result of a shortcoming in your framework.

Keep in mind that systems and procedures that worked in your company's early stages may not work on a larger scale when perfecting processes. As you create, you'll need to change processes, which is where flexibility and versatility become major.

The way to scaling a business and shaping a strong center is laying out a structure of what worked and kept your business moving along as expected in the early years.

You can continuously develop this center as you develop, however whenever you've reached a specific level, it's difficult to reproduce.

5. Establish your team:

Although it may seem obvious, scaling a business requires a strong team. While figuring out how to scale a business, one of the main viewpoints is making a supervisory group that is versatile and can develop with it.

Notwithstanding, your group incorporates something other than your representatives. Foster outer associations with accomplices, providers, and different associations that add to your general development to economically scale a business.

Also, recall your client base, which is one more center colleague. Quite possibly of the best thing about working an independent venture is laying out close connections with your clients and giving them your desired insight from start to finish.

A definitive goal is to develop an intense fan base that will advance your image and help in business extension through verbal.

Keep in mind, the local area you make around your developing business can support your establishment, strength and influence. Having a strong organization is important for the meaning of scaling a business, so get some margin to fabricate a group to impel you into what's in store.

6. Learn when to delegate tasks so that you can work "on" the business rather than "in" it.

In the event that you have major areas of strength for a, you ought to have sufficient trust to designate significant errands.

Notwithstanding, as an entrepreneur, you need to feel engaged with each part of your organization and may experience issues giving up in specific regions.

A significant piece of figuring out how to extend a business is utilizing endeavors.

What are you doing that another person could deal with?

Try not to exchange your time for dollars. Your business must have the option to run itself and flourish in any event, when you're not there. Do this by tending to restricting convictions, for example, "assuming I need something done well, I need to do it without anyone else's help," and by laying out assignment propensities that permit you to possess your time.

7.   Fabricate your Image:

Scaling a business requires realizing your identity as an organization: What can you provide your clients?

In what ways would you differ from the opposition?

What isolates you from others?

What are your most unmistakable shortcomings?

For what reason would you say you are so strong?

What is it that you really need to say?

How might you cause an adjustment of your industry?

It could require a long time to respond to these inquiries, so begin with an essential system and work from that point.

More modest organizations are preferred ready to switch gears over enormous enterprises, so on the off chance that another procedure is required, make the most of the chance to enhance and adjust.

Remember that as you develop, your organization's way of life will be impacted by your image.

It will set the norm for making your recruits and laying out the client experience you need. It will moreover influence your association's advancing, arrangements, and plan attempts.

8. Connect With your Customers:

Scaling a business is pointless if it doesn't produce devoted customers. It is vital for your business' progress amidst moving purchaser inclinations to develop raving devotees of your item. At the point when an organization is developing, it goes through a hatching stage during which it can test methodologies for laying out and keeping up with client connections as well as practices that are fixated on the necessities of the client in each part of the business.

To cultivate a cooperative culture of development, you believe each colleague should show compassion, regard, and transparency.

From that point, everybody on staff can construct a compatibility with your clients, making associations that will assist your item with selling itself.

9. Work on your Systems administration Abilities:

You've likely heard the platitude, "no man is an island." This piece of shrewdness is exceptionally valid for business visionaries, who should create and develop an immense organization of partners, business mentors, assets and tutors to interface them with the perfect individuals to guarantee proceeded with development. While figuring out how to scale a business, go to business organizing capabilities and join an industry-related bunch for proceeding with instruction and expert associations. It's likewise useful to engage in private or business training and associate with those business veterans about turning into your guide. Scaling a business is definitely not a lone undertaking — the more individuals you have on your side, the more fruitful you will be.

10.   Prioritize Sustainability:

Creativity is essential for any business, but making snap decisions when running a business is not appropriate.

Rather than being a wide open device for critical thinking, consider imagination a procedure for growing a business.

Focusing on maintainable development assists you with moving toward difficulties mindfully and track down arrangements that help your organization's drawn out prosperity.

11.   If you have reached a plateau, scaling will appear to be impossible.

Proceed to adjust and improve. It is always possible to learn how to scale a business, so if that is how it feels, it is time to alter your strategy. When was the most recent time your company prioritized innovation? When was the most recent time you evaluated and confronted the obstacles preventing your business from progress? In business and life, in the event that you're not developing, you're kicking the bucket. Change your company for the sake of change; strategically aligning your choices with your ultimate goal will make it easier to grow your business.

Be careful and take as much time as is needed.

Embrace a triumphant outlook yet be careful as you do as such. Keep in mind that rapid expansion is one thing, but steady expansion is what makes a business last.

CONCLUSION

As we arrive at the last pages of "Sales Wizardry: Unlocking Sales Potential," it's time to take stock of the amazing journey we've shared. Throughout this magical journey, you must have developed strong relationships, mastered communication, mastered persuasion, and successfully overcame objections.

Presently, old buddy, now is the ideal time to embrace your internal arrangements wizard. You have the data, capacity, and sureness to investigate the arrangement scene like never before.

You have the ability to enamor possibilities, close arrangements with artfulness, and scale your deal endeavors for long haul achievement.

Bearing in mind, being a business wizard isn't only about the procedures and techniques you've learned. It's tied in with embracing your own extraordinary style, mixing your own touch into each communication, and allowing your energy to radiate through. Trust in your capacities, have confidence in the worth you bring, and let your inward arrangements wizard guide you to significance.

As you set out on your future deals tries, recall the examples you've advanced inside these pages. Remain inquisitive, proceed to learn and develop, and hone constantly your art. The universe of deals is consistently developing, and as an arrangements wizard, you have the ability to adjust and flourish.

Thus, old buddy, go forward with certainty and embrace your internal arrangements wizard. May your deals process be overflowing with captivating victories, enchanted associations, and boundless conceivable outcomes. You have the ability to accomplish extraordinary things within yourself.